Be Friendship Focused

EASY-TO-FOLLOW MANUAL

A small-group program for anti-bullying and peer conflict-resolution through self-empowerment and social skills development

(Grades 3-8)

By Kristine Rose Grant, MA, PPS, LMFT

youth light inc.

© 2011 by YouthLight, Inc.
Chapin, SC 29036

All rights reserved.
Permission is given for individuals to reproduce
the activities and worksheet sections in this book.
Reproduction of any other material is strictly prohibited.

Cover Design and Layout by Diane Florence
Project Editing by Susan Bowman

ISBN: 978-1-59850-098-1

Library of Congress Number
2011920212

10 9 8 7 6 5 4 3 2 1
Printed in the United States

Table of Contents

© YouthLight, Inc.

Table of Contents

© YouthLight, Inc.

Introduction

At last, a very "user friendly" guide for teachers, counselors, and other child mentors that offers clear and easy, step-by-step instructions for leading a successful group process that helps children to reduce negative behaviors and enhance positive social interactions. More importantly, through this Be Friendship Focused (BFF) group encounter, children learn ways to create a positive sense of personal power that can sustain them through life. Included in the BFF Group manual are philosophical overviews that explain concepts and goals; scripted samples that are helpful to refer to when presenting ideas; creative and fun group exercises; and sample forms.

Our children are invaluable. The course of society is predicated by the character and values of its people. There is a growing deep concern regarding relational aggression and the terrible life-long effects of this upon our children's sense of happiness and achievement in school. Within our schools, there is an urgency to fulfill a commitment that complies with set standards for education. All too often, educational pursuits are stymied when children encounter emotional set backs or turmoil, when they feel overwhelmed, and when they are in despair. If a child does not feel socially accepted, physically and emotionally safe, or if a child feels that in order to survive the school's social climate, he or she must compromise personal values and good behavior; and if a child's feelings of self-worth or personal foundation is weak, his or her ability to learn may be compromised. Therefore, a response to intervention or RTI method must be considered and implemented.

The underlying premise that fuels the outcome of the BFF group is the understanding that all forms of bullying whether acts of verbal or physical aggression, psychological intimidation, and/or social exclusion, stem from the participant's lack of positive self-regard or true sense of personal strength. The term "participants" refers to the "bully," the "target" and the "bystander(s)."

The BFF experience allows group leaders to both inform and actively engage with students, so they may gather insights such as recognizing bullying and other forms of relational aggression, as well as understanding the underlying root cause of engaging in acts of bullying. More importantly, as a result of participating in the BFF group, its members will derive a deep sense

 # Introduction

of satisfaction from strengthening personal resiliency, formulating an improved positive self-image, obtaining a better sense of social connectedness, and gaining a real working knowledge of possibilities for realizing personal and educational goals.

"Personal Power" or self-confidence that promotes positive personal achievement, in turn, begets more self-confidence. This is the "positive feedback loop" found within the BFF: Be Friendship Focused encounter. The running theme or underlying goal is that self-confidence can carry each student through a more enriched, self-actualized, or satisfying life that contributes toward moral sustenance and overall social evolvement. Self-confidence includes having a sense of confidence in the future, in the classroom, amongst family, and in building and maintaining healthy friendships. Self-confidence is synonymous with emotional survival. A healthy self-confidence allows children to reach out to others, to care, to be hopeful, to make sound decisions, to dream, and to dare to be their best.

It is a privilege to share the concepts, and group exercises included in this manual. Each group leader who lends their precious time, energy, and heart-felt intention toward helping our children learn to recognize their own bright light, to allow it to shine even in the shadows; must know that you have initiated an unfoldment of kindness and personal power that will enrich our world and be "paid forward" over and over again. It has been said, "Students will not remember teachers for academic lessons; rather, students will remember them for the life lessons that involve humanity and dignity."

Please contact me at www.kristinerosegrant.com or e-mail me at k.rosegrant@att.net should you have questions about how to administer this program. Thank you for your amazing contribution to our youth.

In gratitude,
Kristine Grant

To my daughter, Alana Joy,
the inspiration for this manual–

May you always shine in the
rainbow's light of
kindness and love...the colors
of your heart.

BFF: Be Friendship Focused

LET'S GET STARTED!

The initial group member meeting of the BFF members is quite important as part of the initiation process to set the overall tone for the group experience. Therefore, it is essential for group leaders to impart a sense of warmth, welcome, and safety, while piquing the members' interest for participation in ongoing group activities or discussions.

Children are sensitive to how they are treated. Depending on their perceived social/emotional status, the BFF group members may be particularly aware of whether or not they feel respected and accepted. As in any similar setting, member participation directly correlates with the level of caring conveyed by the leader. The atmosphere in which the group is held should encourage each member's full participation. Therefore, leaders are encouraged to embrace each individual member with a sense of kindness, patience, and positive regard. Try not to focus upon a student's history or reputation. Rather, approach the BFF group as a remarkable opportunity to celebrate each child's uniqueness along with a sense of gratitude for what is about to unfold!

Each individual BFF group will cultivate its' own personality or group synergy. What occurs within the group experience may be somewhat predictable as far as promoting group goals, but the synergistic process and individual/group evolvement is part of what makes leading groups such as this so interesting and rewarding. The following steps outline the initial BFF group meeting.

SETTING THE STAGE

WHO: Group Leaders: As mentioned previously, the only imperative for the group facilitator is to preferably be affiliated with a school, church, community organization, or private practice, and have a genuine interest and appreciation for children. Anyone who realizes the excessive stress so many children experience today and truly wishes to help make a difference can proudly and easily lead a BFF group!

WHO: Group Members: Potential BFF group members may be referred by their parent, a teacher, other mentor or self-referred. A BFF group constellation may consist of children who are

BFF: Be Friendship Focused

considered aggressive or have a reputation for being "Bullies," children who are attention seeking or gravitate toward involvement in social scenes, i.e. "Drama Queens or Kings," children who consider themselves to be harassed or victimized by others or "Targets," children who tend to be "Followers," or fail to stand up to bullies for fear of rejection or victimization, otherwise known as "Bystanders," children who tend to be invisible, isolate themselves, or are considered "Loners," or any other child who may benefit from building a stronger, more positive sense of self.

Group size may vary; however, four to six children per group is recommended. If the group is larger, the time allotment per session may be increased up to one hour. It is recommended that groups do not exceed ten children. Larger groups of 8 to 10 members may benefit from a co-facilitator or group assistant.

The BFF group process is ideal for single-gender groups (boys or girls) of approximately the same age. All of the following group processes described in this manual are designed to effectively capture the interest of participants and ignite a perceptual shift or to glean a new understanding that promotes social/emotional growth. While at least one of the group processes is gender specific, similar outcomes are sought regardless of the group's gender composition.

WHAT:

The BFF group format is designed to allow for ten (10) sessions altogether. The first session is a "pre-group" meeting with parents and teacher(s). This is followed by eight (8) separate group sessions that include the group facilitator and members only. The final session is an "after-care" meeting whereby the group leader meets with parents and teacher(s) to discuss/share the progress of each member as well as the overall efficacy of the group process. Your BFF graduates (the children) may be included and may wish to share their completed final project with the group. Recommendations for continued progress for each student should be shared with parent(s) and/or teacher(s).

The BFF group process is formatted with easy step-by-step directions that allow for a 45-50 minute session. The group leader will need a few minutes to make sure the room is prepared in advance and another few minutes after each session to notate any points of interest that occurred within the session.

 © YouthLight, Inc.

BFF: Be Friendship Focused

WHERE: BFF groups do not necessarily have to be held at a school site. Organizations such as the YMCA, Boys and Girls Club, parks and recreation center, local church or synagogue, etc., may also be considered to host a BFF group. As mentioned previously, anyone who realizes the excessive stress so many children experience today and truly wishes to help make a difference can proudly and easily lead a BFF group!

The BFF group setting ideally is held in a comfortable, well lit room with sufficient seating and a table. Placement of chairs in a circular fashion is usually ideal. A table placed in the center may be beneficial, especially if snacks are provided or for certain group assignments. Whether food or beverages are provided is up to the group leader's discretion. Offering a snack may help group members feel more at ease about being in the group. Healthy snacks such as sliced apples with cinnamon or other fruits, raw vegetables and dip, cheese, popcorn, granola bars, raw almonds, or other dried fruit snacks such as "fruit roll-ups" may be considered. Drinks such as water, juice, herbal teas, or hot chocolate are optional. It's best to avoid heavily processed or sugary foods or beverages. When food and beverages are provided, remember to have an enough plates, cups, napkins as well as an accessible waste can for easy refuse.

HOW: In order to formulate a BFF group, the leader must have students referred for the program; parents must provide informed consent; and the prospective group members must be made aware of their referral and/or acceptance into the group. If a teacher is planning to hold a BFF group, he or she may already have certain students in mind or the school administrator, counselor, school nurse or any other support staff member may refer students. Otherwise, if there is not a "built in" referral system, the group leader may advertise for a BFF group through flyers, Internet, school or local newspaper, parent-newsletter, media center, or after-school program schedule of events.

The goals of the BFF process are founded upon truth, kindness and compassion for oneself and others. BFF group leaders play a role in truly helping young people achieve life skills that enable an open heart, genuine self-confidence, and positive outlook that leads to empathy, respect and acceptance of others. All of this supports the positive energy necessary for creating a beautiful life. This way of "being" forges a social dynamic that ensures a better future for our society. It is an honor, in deed, to gift the young with an opportunity to acquire the attributes of kindness along with a vision for amazing possibilities.

Ready to Begin

PRE-SESSION PARENT/TEACHER MEETING

Before your initial BFF group session begins, it is important to enlist the parents or caretakers in their child's process. The importance of parent involvement cannot be stressed enough. Parents are the first teachers. Their own social/emotional style is passed down to their offspring to one degree or another. How a parent models their behavior under social stress or circumstance is easily learned by their children. For example, an aggressive or authoritarian-style parent may inadvertently weaken their child's self-concept or self-efficacy. A parent with a more passive demeanor may teach their child that their needs are not important or that it is not okay to stand up for yourself.

A parent's attitude or how they perceive daily life is absorbed by their children. If a parent maintains a philosophy that life is difficult, or they often maintain a negative outlook, tend to withhold affection, function from a sense of fear and lack hope, faith, and trust, their children more often form similar perceptions. The family history or ongoing issues may also have a negative impact on a child's outlook or sense of security. Generally, it is not the parent's intention to cause emotional harm to their child. However, too often, parents feel overwhelmed and may lack a healthy self-esteem or confidence in their role as parents and their ability to provide a healthy lifestyle, emotionally or otherwise, for their family.

While the teachings that may be gleaned by children through the BFF group process alone are quite beneficial and can be amazing and carry positive life-long effects, if the parents can be enlightened even to a small degree through this process, and can support their child's participation and group commitment, the success of the BFF group is markedly enhanced even further.

There are many ways to contact parents and share the vision and benefits of the BFF group. One suggestion is to hold a parent/teacher group meeting whereby the BFF group particulars are introduced and questions or concerns addressed.

1. Send home an invitation to the parents of prospective members (See parent/teacher meeting sample in back section of this manual).

 © YouthLight, Inc.

Ready to Begin

2. Be sure to provide some refreshments at this meeting. Whether prospective members have been referred by the site administrator due to a child's social maladjustment; school disciplinary file; a Student Study Team referral; by another concerned staff member; or by the parents themselves, it is important to "level the playing field" at this gathering. In other words, do not discuss any particular child's issues or history. You may invite parents to contact you at a later date in order to share meaningful information regarding their child's history and ongoing concerns.

3. Inform the group about the goals, group process, confidentiality, and commitment toward attendance and participation.

EXAMPLE OF INFORMATION PROVIDED AT PARENT/TEACHER PRE-SESSION GATHERING

This includes the introduction, explanation of group goals, process, and parent survey on page 68.

 ### SAMPLE INTRODUCTION /PARENT-TEACHER INTAKE

"Welcome to the introduction to our BFF Be Friendship Focused group process. My name is.......,(name and title), I am so very excited to meet you and to work with your children, in order to help them achieve mastery over their lives in the most positive, effective way. Today's society is often complex, competitive, and arduous. So much is asked of our kids regarding school and social success that it can often be overwhelming, or at times, even traumatizing. Sometimes, our kids may make poor choices or discover coping mechanisms that are detrimental to their own personal identity and individual greatness. The goal of the BFF (Be Friendship Focused) group process is to help children develop a stronger personal foundation, be more resilient, deal with stress more effectively, instill a very optimistic outlook and allow for a deeper sense of happiness and personal satisfaction. To emphasize, the goals of BFF are to provide life-long tools for personal empowerment that will carry over through future experiences and endeavors."

Ready to Begin

SS "We will be involved in different exercises and processes that are not intimidating, and never depreciating. Rather, each process is designed to invigorate the member's imagination, creativity, and self-acceptance. Actually, the children really enjoy these rather fun, engaging group activities and projects. While children are encouraged to participate; they are never judged or pushed to lend input. However, they must commit to regular attendance. Each session's process builds upon the next; therefore, it is essential to gain the most benefit by attending each session."

"I applaud each of you for being here tonight. This tells me how truly connected you are or wish to be to your child. When a child feels a healthy connection to his/her parent or caretaker, there is less likelihood of a child rebelling or acting out. And so our group will unfold with a sense of gratitude imparted by your commitment and willingness to provide this rewarding opportunity. I hope that, over the next two months, you will take note of any changes in your child's behavior or outlook. I encourage you to discuss your child's group experiences with him or her and to strengthen their participation with positive reinforcements in the form of verbal acceptance and praise. My telephone number is……. Feel free to contact me with any concerns or questions you may have."

All members are encouraged to maintain confidentiality within the group. This enhances a sense of group identity, safety, and connection. However, they are allowed to discuss any personal occurrence or lend feed-back that pertains to their own experience with you. If anyone discloses something that could be harmful to them or others I will need to report this information to the principal, counselor or social worker.

Are there any questions so far?

Thanks for such excellent questions. I'm sure the other parents were wondering the same thing. I'd like to ask you to complete the Parent Survey I'm about to hand out before you leave this evening, so that I may have a clearer understanding of your child's positive strengths as well as what they may be struggling with. In approximately 9 weeks, or after the completion of this BFF group, we will meet once again to discuss members' progress and any future recommendations."

Congratulations! You have just completed the first step of the BFF Group.

(Afterwards, provide the parent survey on page 68 and make sure it is completed before the meeting adjourns).

SESSION 1

1. Welcome:

First, extend a warm welcome to each group member, individually. Introduce yourself as their BFF group leader. You may have them sign the attendance roster. You may wish to provide name tags.

2. The Buy In:

In this part, you will actually solicit the advantages for personal gain that will be provided by completing a BFF group.

An example or sample script, (**) is used throughout the book to assist you:**

 "I am so pleased and excited to see each of you here. This is a huge opportunity to become a much more empowered person. Does anyone know the difference between "being powerful and being empowered? Being "powerful" can just mean coming on strong, but being "empowered" means that you know how to direct or use your power to create good things. Leaders are empowered people. Is there anyone here who doesn't want to be more popular or thought of as a leader? You want to be popular because you're well liked as a true friend who really cares and not just because you have a label, like being "cool" for the wrong reasons. If you really pay attention— that is, listen well, participate, and come to each session, you will be surprised at how much happier you will become or how much more empowered you will feel. You might even notice that other kids want to be more like you. We will be meeting each week at this time for seven more sessions after today, so you can consider the BFF group as your own "club."

"We will be sharing ideas and creating some fun projects during our sessions. This group is actually like a wonderful gift to you. At the end of our last meeting, you might find yourself feeling quite differently. Your attitudes and opinions about some things, or how you experience life might shift or change. Our goal is to make this a really fun and great experience for you. Everything you learn, will serve you for the rest of your life."

SESSION 1

"I am only going to ask you the following: Keep an open mind, share if you can, have fun, be respectful of yourself and others, and come to each session. Oh, there is one more thing that is called "Confidentiality." Does anyone know what that means? Anything that is discussed in our BFF group stays within the group." (Explain the concept clearly and give examples that are not too negative such as: "If someone says they don't know how to swim, or they are afraid in the dark, we don't tease them or gossip about it to others.) You might discuss what personally happened during a BFF session for you, or talk about your own experiences of the group with your parents or family. But it is very important to know that you can keep a promise to one another here and that is: What we share that is personal is not shared outside of our group."

Setting Guidelines for Respectful Behaviors During Group

Make sure each member understands what behaviors are expected during each group session as well as what is not allowed. In order to maintain mutual respect and teach children better listening and sharing skills, it is important to clearly impart certain rules of behavior. The following are suggestions for this: **"Let's first discuss other rules for good BFF behaviors."**

- No talking when someone else is sharing. Often, this can be a challenge for certain youngsters who enthusiastically wish to lend verbal input without permission while another member is speaking. A "manipulative" such as a squeeze ball, wand, or any simple object may be utilized for permission to share. The use of a manipulative allows anyone holding the object to have permission to speak. Once they have finished sharing, they can return the object to the group leader or give it to another member who also desires to share. The emphasis on this is that no one, (other than the group leader), may speak without holding the "manipulative." Or you may simply require a member to raise his/her hand when wishing to share with the group. Let members know in advance that everyone will be given an opportunity to share.

- The "I pass" rule: This lets members know that no one is ever forced to answer or verbally share with the group. If a member is reluctant to verbalize, they can simply say "I pass." This "I pass" rule creates a better sense of safety. It allows members to relax, and even if a member is not verbalizing, he/she will still benefit from the group process. In my experience, it is rare

that a member chooses to "pass" on an opportunity for sharing. However, for example, if a child has had a previous experience of speaking out at the expense of feeling humiliated or publicly shamed, naturally, he/she will most likely feel a sense of dread when called upon to share. Over time, this type of social anxiety should fade, as a more light-hearted self-concept emerges along with the idea that it is "okay to make mistakes" and other acts of forgiveness are developed.

- No talking with others, unless it is shared with the group. It is not only respectful, but important for each member to fully pay attention and participate in each exercise as much as possible. Each member should understand that their presence is a very important element not only for personal gain, but to the growth of fellow members. Again, the power manifested through this group process grows larger within total group awareness.

- Staying seated: Members need to know that permission must be granted before getting up from his/her seat. Be sure to reinforce adherence to BFF group behavior rules by positive feedback, acknowledgement, and gratitude.

- Refreshments: Other rules regarding partaking in refreshments are up to each group leader's discretion. Personally, I allow simple healthy snacks and a beverage to be consumed during the group process.

INTRODUCTIONS: Members Begin to Share

First, begin by inquiring with each member about their personal view of life. You may consider inquiring about any number of interests or concerns i.e. about their family, how many children, what number are they, etc. This may be followed by eliciting opinions and other sharing by asking open-ended questions such as:

"When do you recall being successful or proud of something you did? What are the key ingredients to being a friend? What do you look for in finding a friend? What is your definition of bullying? Has anyone been a bully or been bullied by someone else? What did that feel like? What is the reason you think that happened?

SESSION 1

What do you enjoy about being at school? What is your favorite hobby? What are your plans for the future? What was the happiest time of your life? If you had a younger sister or brother, what would you tell them about how to be a friend to others?

Obviously, there are an infinite number of questions or topics that can be discussed during this introductory period.

- Discussion of feelings and how feelings are actually felt in the body:

SS "Do you remember a time when you felt nervous, angry, embarrassed, happy, joyful, or excited? What did that feel like? When you feel really happy about something, what does that feel like in your body? Have you ever been so excited you can't wait for something, like waiting to open a present or go to a party? How did it feel when you did something really terrific, like win a game or first ride a bike? Or describe a time your mom or dad was really proud of you?" (Ask members to share feelings of satisfaction, safety, and happiness.)

SS "Now, let's talk about feeling uncomfortable and what that might mean. Has anyone ever felt butterflies, or knots in their stomach, or felt warm, like their face was turning red, or their palms sweating? You might have felt like this when you were embarrassed, ashamed, nervous, or angry. Everything we feel in our body is connected to how we feel emotionally."

Lead into a discussion regarding physical feelings and how they relate to emotional states. Emphasize the relationship between, our mind, our body, and our emotions.

SS "We are all connected to our mind, body, and heart — or our feelings. I would like to demonstrate an example of what I mean":

SESSION 1

Exercise: Mind-Body-Emotions - Muscle Testing

Demonstrate and explain with one volunteer who holds his/her non-dominant (usually the left) arm out perpendicular to the side. Test the resistant strength of the volunteer with light hand or two-finger pressure on the forearm. Demonstrate resistance when you say something positive to the child, such as "I really like you….You have pretty hair….Wow, you are strong…You look very smart, etc." Notice, the arm can solidly resist the pressure. Then, you may demonstrate a lack of muscle resistance with a negative phrase such as "I am angry with you, or you seem weak." You will notice the arm usually loses its' strength.

It is important to let the group know that what is being said here is just to show each other how words can wound or weaken your physical and emotional strength. Have BFF members pair up and demonstrate this (mind-body-emotions) muscle testing – one pair at a time – performing this exercise. This is a visceral exercise that demonstrates a point. This exercise should easily lead into a discussion regarding how words can affect someone physically. You may share that there is scientific evidence that shows sickness or dis-ease is often associated with negative feels such as anger, sadness, or being resentful. Even when someone says a negative remark about themselves during this exercise, their own arm will tend to weaken or drop.

SESSION 2

"As I Believe, I Am."

Share any stories of how members chose to react or respond to a stressful situation. Stress the point of having POWER THROUGH CHOOSING. Discuss emotional states, for example, if someone talks of being angry; distill the emotion down to other feelings states such as:

"It sounds like you are actually feeling hurt, sad, frustrated, or disappointed." (Then stress the platitude of having the power to choose your experience.) "Did you know that no matter what is occurring, or how bad a situation may be, we each have the power to choose how we experience that? In other words, we choose how we respond or react emotionally to everything. So you can actually decide whether you want to let something that happens make you feel really upset, or you can decide not to let it bother you too much. I would like to have us share an experience with our group, so that we can really start to see how this works."

Exercise: The Best Birthday Party

Step 1: Have members close their eyes and consider that tomorrow morning when they awake, it would actually be their birthday. Have members think about what the most perfect birthday celebration would be like. Let members know that there are no limitations, but to think about how their birthday would be celebrated if they could have it be anything they want. What would make them feel the most loved and honored by their friends and family?

Step 2: Allow a few minutes for each member to really imagine where the celebration would take place, who would be present, what gifts might be received, what favorite foods, flavor of cake, game activities, what wish would be made when blowing out the candles, how he/she feels when guests are singing the "happy birthday song," etc.

Step 3: After a few minutes are allowed for each member to fully imagine the most "perfect" birthday celebration, invite each member to share what their celebration would be like.

SESSION 2

Step 4: Have members close their eyes once again and imagine one party guest saying the following statement, "I am really not having a very good time here." Ask each member to consider what that would feel like and consider how they would respond both verbally and emotionally.

Step 5: Ask each member to share that imagined experience.

Step 6: A teachable moment

- Stress the point about the ability to choose your reaction to this situation, as well as any other, by being more compassionate. In consideration of this particular unhappy party guest, for example; rather than reacting in a negative way such as thinking: "This guest doesn't like ME or is trying to make ME feel bad, or trying to ruin MY party," another possibility, is to consider that this guest is uncomfortable right now, but it really has nothing to do with you. Explain that this is usually the case. We may imagine they're not having a good time because they don't like us or the party we planned; when actually, the problem is something else such as they have a stomach ache, they are feeling shy, or they don't know how to do an activity you planned.

- One response might be: "I am sorry you feel that way, but I am sure glad you came to my party. It means a lot to have my friends here." Or "Please try to enjoy yourself; we are going to play a fun game or have cake soon." Or "Sorry you feel that way; would you help me serve the ice cream though?"

 Although we are never responsible for another's happiness, we can show caring and concern. It is important to understand that we always choose or decide how we feel. When we are happy and we feel really good about ourselves, it is so much more difficult to be upset by another's feelings or actions. While we only get to celebrate our birthday once a year, we can still choose to feel like we're celebrating every day. It begins with being kind to ourselves. The party guest, who feels unhappy and complains they are not having a good time, has also made a choice. They may choose to believe something negative such as "No one likes me; I hate parties because I get bored; I have nothing to say to anyone; I feel like a nerd."

SESSION 2

- "When we are "kind," how does that make us feel? The seat of our emotions shines from within the heart. We can become more powerful and uplift our immediate experience by expanding our heart's energy field. (Demonstrate the open heart with arms outward arching…..Discuss when we choose to BE or REMAIN hurt or angry….how that also affects the heart energy center by collapsing it. (Demonstrate visual arms folding inward). The adage, "Share the Love" refers to how we can expand the energy in our environment. And when good energy is expanded or grows outward, we begin to attract like-energy. Other people start to feel really good and are drawn to be around us." (Ask a BFF member to describe something that makes him/her feel really happy or excited, then ask him/her to talk about something that they dread or that makes them sad. Follow up by asking the other group members how they felt listening to these variations.

- What does "compassion" mean? It means to understand and be concerned about the suffering of another person. When you are showing compassion, you want to help the other person to feel or do better.

- Share BFF POWER CARDS. Have each member choose one or more cards to read aloud and open to group discussion.

- Discuss homework assignment on "random acts of kindness (3 separate acts of unsolicited kindness to another.) This particular homework assignment encourages each member to take a "risk" in offering an act of kindness with no personal gain in mind. These acts of kindness may be toward a family member, teacher, or friend. However, at least one act of kindness must be toward someone they do not know or do not know well, such as helping an elderly person to cross the street, or inviting another student who is not your friend to play, or standing up for someone who is being bullied etc.

 © YouthLight, Inc.

SESSION 3

Part 1: Review homework assignment:

Members share what random acts of kindness they performed. Ask what it felt like to be kind to another for no reason, even when they had nothing to gain. Explain concepts such as: feeling pride, generosity, sympathy, understanding, etc. What happened as a result of this act of kindness? How did the individual receiving this kindness respond? Ask whether members enjoyed this assignment. Encourage them to continue experimenting with this, with a goal of one act of kindness every day.

 ## Exercise: Body Language Awareness - Charades

Part 2: Discuss the concept of Body Language:

 "Did you know that even though we might not say something mean, unkind or disrespectful to another, we show our feelings in other ways? I am going to demonstrate a feeling without saying a word. I would like you to try to guess what I am feeling." The group leader then demonstrates the following gestures:

- Eye rolling
- Scowling
- Nodding head in approval (making eye contact) while clapping hands
- Shaking head with disapproval (narrowing or rolling eyes)
- Folding arms and turning your back
- Opening arms, smiling, giving thumbs up

SESSION 3

1. Have members name and/or describe different emotional states or ways of being.

2. Leader must prepare ahead of time: Cut blank sheet s of paper into squares. Write a different "feeling" on each paper, such as: bored, curious, surprised, happy, funny, ignoring, sorry, approval, disapproval, angry, sad, embarrassed, hurt, frustrated, scared, confused, excited, bossy, etc. Fold each paper in half and put in a box or bag, so the children can pick one out later.

3. Have each member take a folded paper. Without disclosing what is written, have members act out these feelings in pantomime, gestures, and facial expressions without words and ask other members to guess what feeling the person is displaying by their body language.

After this exercise, reiterate the concept that our Body Language is used as a tool for conveying how we feel. Ask members to share their experiences when they remember someone using body language. This is followed by a discussion on how our body language also speaks a message to others, just as words do.

 ## Exercise: Teach ZIP-UP

 "Have any of you ever learned martial arts or have you ever seen a martial arts performance live or on TV? Perhaps you are learning Karate or Kung Fu or one of the other martial arts? You may have noticed that the opponents often swing their arms around, and may use a big sweeping gesture with their hands. Like when Karate masters break bricks in half with the side of their palm. (Demonstrate a martial arts type of motion raising hand and sweeping it across and downward similar to a slashing gesture)."

"The martial arts are about the art of focus and channeling of your own energy. That energy is directed toward overcoming the opponent. This "energy" gives them physical strength or power. Actually, martial artists often try to weaken their opponent by cutting into their energy field with a slicing type of movement. In order to win, the opponent must be aware of and maintain his or her own energy. The same idea holds true for everyone. We can weaken someone by cutting into their energy field."

SESSION 3

"We can also weaken their energy by directing negativity toward them. We know we can hurt someone physically and with words. We can also hurt someone with our body language. For example, when we give someone a 'mean' or 'dirty' look such as rolling our eyes, giving a "mad-dog" stare, or looking down on someone in disapproval with our eyes. Just as there are many ways we can make each other feel better, and give them a feeling that they are accepted, there are also many ways people can hurt or weaken another's energy field just by giving them a certain look. However, I will teach you how to protect your energy or how to keep yourself "energized" so things others say or do won't affect you as much."

Step One: Group leader stands and gestures with a single arm sweeping motion. Begin by sweeping the arm in an upward motion as if zipping your jacket, all the way up to the forehead. This is called the Zip-Up.

Step Two: Allow BFF group members to practice the Zip-Up.

SS "You can use this exercise anytime. It looks like you are greeting someone, waving a big "hello," when actually; you are keeping your energy field protected. Another way to maintain your energy is to cross your arms and/or cross your legs like you are protecting yourself. You might do this if you are being confronted in a negative way by someone, for example, if someone says something negative or mean to you, or you feel like someone does not like you. Just by doing this reminds us to maintain our energy and not allow someone else to take our power."

SS "Now that we have had a chance to see how we communicate feelings without necessarily using words, think about how other people experience our body language. For example, what might it be like to teach students in a class when they are not looking at the teacher, placing their head on the desk, or looking out the window? What might it be like for your mom or dad when they ask you to do something and you resist? How do you communicate with them?"

SESSION 3

🌸 Exercise: Impromptu Skits for Compassionate Understanding

- Have a member act like a teacher lecturing to the class, while the group leader demonstrates ways of acting like a student that are disrespectful such as ignoring, looking away, yawning, placing head on desktop, doodling on paper, making sounds, slumping in seat, rolling eyes, etc. Then ask the group to share their insights and ask the student pretending to be the teacher what it felt like to be disrespected.

- Members usually enjoy these impromptu skits, so time permitting, you might repeat this exercise by having another member act like a parent or caretaker. Again, the group leader responds with disrespectful behaviors such as talking back, ignoring, scowling, complaining, etc.

Revisit the idea that our emotions convey messages both through oral language and nonverbal body language; and how we express ourselves with a combination of vocal tone, facial expressions, posturing, inflection etc. Encourage the group to think about how body language also contributes to the shift of energy. For example, when one student is disrespectful during class, the teacher has to stop the lesson to deal with the rude, misbehaving student. Then other students start talking while the teacher is reprimanding the rude one and this disrupts the learning. How can we use our body language to have more positive energy?

Journaling: Instruct BFF members to begin journaling their experiences with BFF group assignments.

- Clarifying or realizing goals through focus and intention using Creative Visualization Techniques

  Discuss the power of "feeling" a desired outcome or allowing something "even better" to manifest or occur through the use of positive visualization, affirmation, writing it down, laughter, anticipation, and other joyful feelings.

 © YouthLight, Inc.

SESSION 3

Exercise: Journaling and Creating Positive Intention

"I encourage each of you to keep a journal. A journal is a blank notebook whereupon you will write your thoughts regarding how you can "Be Friendship Focused." It is your personal journal. You will not be asked to share this with anyone. You are free to write down any words that might encourage you to "stay in your power" or to expand your heart energy by being positive in your thoughts and feelings.

"Writing in a journal is a way to really tune into what you choose to create in your life. What you focus upon, you will attract. If you think about sad or angry thoughts or if you focus upon negative thoughts like, "It is really hard to make friends, I am dumb, no one likes me, my mom is always mad at me"… in a way, you are choosing this as your reality.

Try changing your thoughts to good, upbeat, and positive ideas and you will see that you start to feel as though you already have it. For example, if you were to write down, "I am well liked by others and my teacher is proud of me," you give energy to this idea by feeling and believing as though it already is happening. Then, act as if it is so, (i.e. consider how you might act like a good friend to others). You may discover, over time, your life actually begins to change for the better.

Imagine your positive thought or desire inside a golden light. Feel that in your heart. Be open and thankful for the vision you are creating. This way, you can shift your focus to create more of what you really want. The more you re-read the positive statement you wrote in your journal, imagine it, and feel it as though it already is beginning to happen, the quicker you might see a positive change occur in your life. Remember to be open to a new way of looking at things or doing things and keep

SESSION 3

→ looking forward to some positive changes."

Homework Assignment #1:

Have BFF members write in their journal what qualities they already possess that would attract others to want to be their friend. One prompt might be: "If someone just met you at school for the first time, why would they want to be friends with you?" List all personality and character traits that you really appreciate about yourself. For example, 'I am funny and good at playing softball.' List any other qualities you are working towards being, such as: 'I am a good student and treat all others with respect; not just my good friends.'

→

Homework Assignment #2:

Encourage each member to really think of how they would like their life to be; to consider what is already working, and what they would like to see change for the better. This can only be expressed as a positive intention. Ask each member to write down a simple statement of how they desire to be as a person or what they would like to create for their life. Let them know, this is personal, therefore, they will share this with the group only if they choose to.

SESSION 4

RECEIVING/GIVING: HONORING OURSELVES AND OTHERS

Group Leader: Greet each member with a warm welcome to the fourth session of the BFF: Be Friendship Focused group.

1. Invite each member participant to share any particular "random acts of kindness" performed or encountered since the last session.

SS "Before we share about our journaling assignment from last week, I would like you all to join in the next exercise."

Exercise: The Art of Compliments

SS "Who in our group enjoys receiving praise or compliments? Who is really generous with giving compliments to others? Some of you may be uncomfortable with either giving or receiving a compliment, or both. Some of you may feel awkward or embarrassed when receiving a compliment, especially from another student or person your own age. Some of you may find it hard to believe that the compliment is really true or you may find it difficult to give a compliment to someone else. This might be because you think the other person will feel uncomfortable, or maybe even not trust that you really feel that way, i.e. they might feel like you are just saying it; that you are being phony; that you just want them to compliment you back, or that you want something from them and you are "buttering them up." Maybe you feel that giving a compliment means you think the other person is actually better than you in some way. You might even feel that complimenting someone else is like giving your power away, as if to say "You really are better than me, or I wish I was more like you." Actually, I would like you all to consider compliments, whether giving or receiving one, as a GIFT."

"When we are sincere, that is when we really mean it. Giving and receiving compliments from one another helps us to feel more supported and connected. If you went to the trouble of finding a special gift for someone's party or a holiday, for example, and they either did not open it, or gave it back, or acted as though they did not appreciate the present, how would that make you feel?

SESSION 4

On the other hand, if you gave someone a special present, and they seemed really happy to receive your gift and thanked you for being so generous, thoughtful, or kind; how would that make you feel? (Allow group members to share their understanding of this concept). Now, I would like you to think about what I am going to say to each of you."

- Group leader then addresses each child and gives a genuine compliment based on what you know or observe to actually be true about that person. It is important to really personalize your compliments, make eye contact with the member recipient, and deliver the compliment with sincerity. For example, "Emily, I am so proud of what an amazing runner you are. I know it takes a lot of determination to win a race"; or "Sean, I love to hear you play the piano, you have a great sense of timing. I can tell you must really practice hard" or "Thank you, Toni, for the beautiful flowers. It means so much that you actually grew them from seed. You really have a green thumb!"

- Next, have the group members pair off with the person seated on their right. If there are an uneven number of children in the group, then the group facilitator may pair up with a member as well.

- Each member is told to look directly at the other student with a kind expression. Instruct one of each pair to think of a genuine or true compliment about the other. Take a minute or two. Instruct one of the pair to give a compliment while the other receiving the compliment remains quiet and continues to make eye contact. After a few moments, instruct the child receiving the compliment to acknowledge this with a simple reply of "Thank you." Repeat this exercise, with each pair switching roles. Then each member who received a compliment turns to the next member on his/her right and the exercise is repeated. Repeat this exercise until each member has both given and received a compliment from all.

- Take some time to process this experience. Invite the BFF group to discuss how this felt and whether it was more comfortable with practice. While some members may act or feel some what uncomfortable with this exercise initially, let members know that it may feel a bit "strange" at first, but the "art of giving a compliment" does become easier and feels more natural with practice. Typically, some group members may tend to give superficial

 © YouthLight, Inc.

compliments such as "I like your shirt" or "I think you're cool." Remind the group that all compliments are good. All compliments are a gift. However, the most special present is one that you really put some thought into, whether you gave them "just the right gift" or a genuine compliment from your heart.

- Encourage group members to comment, ask questions, or otherwise discuss this exercise and how the compliment made them "feel." Then imagine how nice it would be to give someone else that same kind of feeling. Remind them that while getting "stuff" such as toys, games, clothes, or gift cards, is always fun, a real compliment is a "gift from the heart" that you can easily find, it doesn't cost anything, and it is always a special and generous gift. Again, remind the members that receiving a compliment with an "open" and thankful heart is actually showing your appreciation and gratitude. Giving compliments to others is a true sign of generosity.

Gratitude: We actually receive more when we are thankful

"When we say "thank you" and actually allow ourselves to accept a compliment, we may find that we start receiving more compliments. You can start being more open to receiving good things in your life when we remember to be thankful or appreciate all that you have already. There is a word for this…it is called "gratitude." In the dictionary, the definition of gratitude is: "a feeling of thankful appreciation for favors or benefits received; thankfulness." I would like you to open your BFF Journal and begin writing down ten things that you are thankful for in your life. (The group leader may wish to give example prompts.)

- Allow time for group members to consider and write down what they are grateful for.

- Inspire the group to consider people in their lives, situations, comforts, freedoms or privileges, health, talents, and anything else that they really appreciate.

- Invite each member to share what they are grateful for. Then inquire about how they "feel" when they become aware of this "state of gratitude."

SESSION 4

- Encourage group members to read their Gratitude List before they go to sleep and upon waking each day. Let them know that they may add to this list as they consider more to be thankful for each day.

DISCRETION IS THE BETTER PART OF VALOR

"We have been talking about what makes us feel good — can anyone name some of the things that make us feel really good about ourselves and our lives?" (Allow time for members' input). "One of the ways we feel good is by giving and receiving positive energy. When we really feel good about ourselves, we do feel happier. We can bring about more positive energy by being kind, being thankful and being in gratitude, and by respecting our selves and others."

"We have already discovered that when we are thoughtful and kind to others, we feel really good or 'energized.' Another really powerful way to be even more 'energized' is when we show kindness, appreciation, respect, or care for ourselves. Kindness, respect, gratitude, and generosity, are all different ways of expressing love. We can love our friends, our family, our school, and ourselves. However, there is a difference between 'bragging' about yourself, or thinking you are somehow better than someone else and truly honoring yourself. Does anyone know the meaning of the word 'honor?' Here are some definitions of the word 'HONOR':

- High regard or great respect given, received, or enjoyed
- A keen sense of right or wrong; (following what is right)
- To show deep respect together with love

We must always honor ourselves in order to be our most powerful. To have good friendships, we must be a good friend; but actually, we must first be a good friend to ourselves. Can anyone share how we might honor ourselves or be our own best friend first? (Allow time for member input.) Let's consider the word Respect and what that really means or really looks like. When we respect others, we show that we are considerate of their feelings, or their beliefs. For example, we already discussed during the first BFF session, how to respect or honor our group experience by listening, being patient, participating as much as we can, promising to maintain confidentiality, and keeping good attendance or coming to each session."

SS "Can anyone name any other ways of being respectful? (Allow for group input.) If we did not show respect by following these rules or conditions for our group, our group would be a lot different, do you agree? (Allow for group input.) What other people in our lives do we show respect to? (Allow for group input.) Your parents, teachers, coaches, the principal — and what about our friends? How do we show respect for our friends?" (Allow for discussion.)

"Okay, now how do we show respect for ourselves?"

(Allow for group discussion, encourage members to talk about respecting their feelings, being able to ask for what they need, how personal hygiene and self-care show self-respect, and putting their best effort towards goals or activities such as trying their best in school or sports or a performance. Taking time for enjoyment of hobbies, talents, joining clubs, volunteering, reading a good book, getting enough rest, eating healthy foods, exercising, being in nature, spending time with family members are also signs of respect for yourself.)

"When you think about what shows self-respect, be sure to consider the difference between what honors our minds, bodies, and spirit and what might be a bad habit or a "way of being" that hides your "light." Hiding your light means you are not fully in your Power. For example, it might be fun to watch a good movie on television; however, if you spend most of your time watching television or playing games on the computer, are you really participating in life? How much time do you spend on the computer instead of playing outdoors or doing other things that show you honor or respect yourself?"

(Allow for group discussion on ways we show self-respect. Encourage members to share about their favorite pastimes; what amount of time is spent watching television, texting or playing on the computer instead of interacting with others.)

SS "It is important to check how and where you spend your time. Where do you focus your energy? Do you spend your time thinking about what is wrong with your life? Do you spend time gossiping or putting someone else down, or thinking how you might get even with someone? Are your thoughts focused on things like, "I am bored, I can't do this, I don't like this or that? What other possible ways could you spend your time that is more fun or interesting?"

SESSION 4

(Open for group discussion on ways to feel better such as helping others, setting/achieving goals, trying or learning something new, etc.).

REVIEW Session 3 Homework Assignment: Ask members to share what they like about themselves and what qualities they have that would make them a good friend. Invite members to include the compliments that they received today in their journals. Allow time for group members to write these comments into their journals.

End Session 4 by reviewing the topics included in today's session such as the gift of giving and receiving compliments; gratitude – or focusing on what we are thankful for; respect – how we treat others. Think about how we respect or honor ourselves.

→ Homework Assignment:

- Continue documenting "Random Acts of Kindness" in your journals.

- Give compliments to 3 people.

- Be aware when or if you receive a compliment this week.

- Write in your journal how you enjoy spending your time. Consider what really "lights you up" or fills you with a sense of joy and excitement.

Time permitting, have each member pull a BFF Power Card.

SESSION 5

CYBER-ISSUES/SELF-CONFIDENCE/THE PROCESS OF FORGIVENESS

Group Leader: Welcome each member with warmth and perhaps a compliment to individual group members or to the group as a whole. Thank the members for receiving your compliment(s) so well.

Share homework assignment from Session 4
(Random acts of kindness; compliments; journal writing; How do you enjoy spending your time?)

Exercise: Crossword Puzzle – Learning Power Words
(Find crossword puzzle on page 64 of BFF Manual)

Engage members in completing the crossword puzzle as a team effort. You might promise the members a special treat or a prize for completing the puzzle. Have a dictionary and thesaurus handy. This is actually a fun exercise and a good way for members to grasp the meaning of words or concepts that apply to what they have already been learning in the BFF group.

VIRTUAL REALITY FRIENDS/INTERNET CONFLICTS DISCUSSION

"Do any of you talk to your friends on the computer? Some people spend so much time making friends on the computer on "My Space" or "Facebook," that they avoid making friends or communicating with people they can talk to or spend time with in person. When we spend time with our friends on the computer, we miss the opportunity of building friendships that are often more real or honest. Enjoying fun experiences with friends is much better than having a computer friendship. Friends you might talk with online might lie or "make-up" stories, or brag about what is not really true about themselves, and they may say things that are mean or unkind about someone because they do not have to face that person in real life."

(Allow time for open group discussion on this matter.)

SESSION 5

 "Some parents will not allow their kids to go online to chat with other children. Do any of you know why? (Allow for group member input.)

Interacting with other people on the computer sometimes can turn out to be a painful experience where someone can have their feelings hurt or their reputation ruined. Sometimes, kids are threatened by bullies on the computer. What someone might say on the computer (which is blasted out to many other children); they probably would not say to someone's face. Somehow on the computer, people often feel they have permission to say things they would never say in person. Has anyone here ever had a bad experience with this on the computer or know of someone else who was gossiped about online?"

(Allow discussion on cyber-bullying knowledge and experience.)

Group leader: At this time, it is important to impart the following concepts to your BFF members:

1. Advise them to NEVER gossip – especially on the computer. Explain why doing so online can be so damaging. Give an example of gossip and how it can hurt someone.

2. Advise them to tell their parents or teacher if they or someone else is being threatened on the computer.

3. Let them know that "what goes around comes around."

4. Emphasize that remarks made on the internet or on "chats" are kept on record and can negatively affect their own reputation.

Taking Responsibility For Your Own Actions

 "Have you ever heard the expression, "what goes around comes around?" What this basically means is that if you give out positive energy such as gratitude, respect, and kindness, you will most definitely begin to receive more of that from others. On the other hand, if you gossip about someone, are somehow mean to another, or do not stand up for yourself or for what is right, you will continue to experience more unhappiness and stress. Can anyone share an experience about this idea?"

(Allow for group member input.)

 © YouthLight, Inc.

SESSION 5

"We talked about cyber-bullies a moment ago and regarding gossiping or saying mean things about someone, or threatening to hurt someone. Whether on the computer or not, being negative or mean will often start a negative cycle and this often ends up with hurt feelings, anger, or even physical fights. Another way to think of this is "Two Wrongs Do NOT Make it Right." Does anyone know what I mean by that expression?"

(Open up for group discussion)

BFF group members are encouraged to discuss their personal experiences of this. In order to process this point further, ask: "What if someone hurt you first such as said something mean to you or about you or threatened you and you did not feel you deserved it? Is it okay to say something mean or ugly to them in response? Or is it okay to threaten someone who has hurt your feelings? Does it make the situation better or worse? Remember….people who act mean toward others are not happy. I know we talked about that at our second meeting when we talked about birthday parties. Do you recall what we learned about why someone might say something that sounds mean?"

(Allow for group member input.)

"Do you recall when we talked about RESPECT? We not only talked about respecting others but to HONOR ourselves with respect. I want you to consider the following idea:"

Self-Confidence = Personal Power

"When we honor ourselves, we take really good care of ourselves. By honoring ourselves, we allow ourselves to become very big, very bright, and very powerful. If we keep ourselves feeling happy and joyful, we feel more powerful and we are CONFIDENT. When we believe in ourselves and our abilities, we have SELF-CONFIDENCE. People that are self-confident radiate a beautiful, powerful energy that attracts positive experiences—including more friendships. Self-confidence begins with feeling really good or positive about ourselves. However, it is more than a feeling, since it becomes a knowing and appreciation of us. Our feelings are the key to what we create in our lives. We must do more than just think—we must know in our heart what is true. Believing in ourselves and knowing that we are a good person, a good friend, and that we try our best to do the right thing, allows us to feel a sense of self-trust or confidence in ourselves, in our friendships, and in our future."

SESSION 5

KEEPING YOUR TANK FULL DISCUSSION

SS "Your personal power comes from your self-confidence...Positive energy, or power, radiates from our heart center and affects our whole being. Let's think of ourselves as a car, for example. While it is important to get your car tuned up regularly by having the oil changed, the tires rotated, new windshield wipers, and such, and it is always nice to ride in a shiny, clean car — you cannot go any where without fuel. Gasoline is the fuel that provides the energy that keeps your car in motion. If you keep the gas tank filled, you know you can pretty much go anywhere. So by keeping your personal tank filled, or being energized, nothing can hold you back either! What do you think are some ways you can keep your personal tank filled or keep yourself energized? We don't run on gasoline, we need a different kind of energy source to stay healthy, confident, and energized. When we are really happy because we feel so good about ourselves and our lives, we are satisfied, our "tank" feels full, and we actually glow with good energy. Happiness and confidence is our fuel."

(Allow for group input – discuss gratitude, kindness, honor, respect, participating in life, etc.)

SS "Sometimes we can feel our personal tank being drained, or that we are losing our energy. When we are sad, afraid, frustrated, angry, or tired – our fuel or energy may start to slow down or empty. That is why it is so important to take good care of ourselves and keep our tanks really full. Again, if our tank is full, and for example, someone says a mean thing or tries to make us feel badly, or we feel left out or become disappointed, we still have the energy to keep moving forward."

HAVE GROUP MEMBERS PULL A POWER CARD and discuss what it means for them.

 © YouthLight, Inc.

SESSION 5

FORGIVENESS

 "Does anyone know the meaning of forgiveness or why it is important to forgive someone who has hurt or disappointed us?"

(Allow for group discussion.)

 "To forgive is to stop being angry and to give up any bad feelings or to stop wanting to punish the person who offended you. Forgiveness is an amazing gift that we give, not only to whoever we are mad at, but more importantly, it is a gift we give to ourselves. When we are angry or upset with someone, is that a good feeling?"

(Allow for group member input.)

 "Do you think it is healthy and good for us to hold onto bad feelings about someone or something that happened in the past? This is called "carrying a grudge." The person you remain angry with or whom you have not forgiven, may not understand how badly you feel and they might not even realize you still are angry with them. In that case, you are the only one suffering. It is like punishing yourself to stay angry with someone. Has anyone ever made a mistake or made a wrong choice? Has anyone done something that they felt badly about or sorry for later? When we make mistakes or when we have made a wrong choice, do we usually learn from that experience?"

(Allow for group input.)

 "Sometimes we not only need to forgive others, but we need to forgive ourselves."

SESSION 5

LETTING IT GO

 "It is a kindness to ourselves and others when we are able to really forgive. It takes a lot of energy to stay mad at someone. And a lot more than it does to forgive. In order to "re-energize your tank," not only should you forgive, but you must let it go for yourself. Sometimes we can really believe that we have forgiven someone for hurting our feelings, but then, later on we think about it again, and find ourselves still feeling angry. If that happens, that means you have not "let it go." Sometimes it takes a while to totally forgive someone. But if our intention or desire is to forgive, and we can bring that into our heart-space, sooner or later we can actually release those bad feelings once and for all. When we feel ashamed or when we have disappointed someone else, although we are really sorry, sometimes it can be hard to forgive ourselves. Can anyone share an experience like that? Can anyone explain how that feels?"

(Open BFF group members to discuss the concept of Forgiveness/Letting Go further).

Teachable Moment

Group Leader: Convey the following important concept or understanding:

 "To forgive ourselves or another is one of the most beautiful gifts you can give. When you truly forgive and let go of any bad feelings you may have, you feel better inside. To learn from mistakes whether our own or another's, gives us power. However, it is also very important to realize although we may forgive someone — we must not allow ourselves to remain victims of further abuse.

 "Do you recall when we talked before about having the power to choose? When we forgive someone, we are making a choice to do so. To be able to release the hurt or the memory of the event and really "let it go," is a process that may take time. It is very important to know that if the same person continues to hurt us or make wrong choices, we may lose our trust in him or her. This holds true if someone is willing and able to forgive you, if you hurt them, whether you meant to or not. For example, if you gossiped about someone or spread rumors, and hurt their feelings, you might feel badly and ask them to please forgive you. But if you continued to talk badly about them, behind their back, then they would lose their trust in your word."

 © YouthLight, Inc.

SESSION 5

Remember: "What goes around eventually comes around." You might be rejected or lose friendships because you are not acting honorably. (Remember to honor means to show respect.) If someone hurt your feelings and continued to hurt you, even after they apologized, you must think about how you can honor yourself, so that they can't keep hurting you. A friendship takes two people, not just one. Again, we all make mistakes, and mistakes are an opportunity to learn what to do or what not to do in the future. But if someone repeatedly disrespects your friendship and does not keep their promise or their word, it is probably wise to end the friendship. Remember, "Two wrongs do not make it right."

SS "Therefore, while you should wish the person offending you well, and you continue to want their happiness, or at least do not wish them any pain, you no longer should interact with them. By removing yourself from harms way or negativity, this is how you may conserve your energy and honor yourself, instead of allowing someone to continue to zap energy from your tank."

(Allow for BFF group member discussion on the concept of: FORGIVENESS/RELEASE/AND LETTING GO OF "TOXIC FRIENDS.")

→ **Homework assignment:** Write about who or what situation you have forgiven in the past; who you still need to forgive; who or what you need to let go of. Think of who has continued to hurt you. Are you allowing anyone to continue to hurt your feelings? What are your choices? When will you be ready to forgive them? What needs to occur before you can forgive? Are you willing to forgive even if no one apologizes to you or understands why your feelings were hurt?

SESSION 6

DRAMA KINGS & DRAMA QUEENS/ PEER PRESSURE VERSUS DOING THE RIGHT THING

Building Resiliency / Send-off Exercise/ Calming Breath / Reframes

Group Leader: Lends a warm welcome to Session number 6 of the BFF: Be Friendship Focused group. Review what was discussed in Session 5: Self-confidence; keeping your tank filled; the power of forgiveness and release; understanding negative patterns and choosing friendship over repeat-offenders.

Ask group members to share homework assignment on journal entries regarding their experiences with forgiveness.

Group Discussion on the Obsession with Drama and/or the Need for Attention

SS "Many of you have had difficult experiences with other kids at school or situations that have happened outside of school that have made you really angry at one time or another. It can be easy to begin to enjoy the attention that we get from others when we talk about upsetting experiences we have had. We often share what happened with others so other kids or adults will feel sorry for us and take our side. Maybe the event was so dramatic (or the way we explain it is dramatic) that others begin to talk about us and about the incident, and then we become an even bigger center of their attention. The focus is on us. We get to receive sympathy. Others might even want to defend us. This can lead to a lot of other people building a dislike or anger toward the person we have had a problem with. This usually leads to more gossip, more anger toward that other person, and often can result in someone getting hurt either emotionally or physically."

"When we gather support for our side from other kids who then "gang-up" on someone we are mad at – what might happen then?"

(Allow for group input and discussion.)

SESSION 6

"So what I am hearing is that the other person's life could become pretty miserable. (Discuss various negative repercussions that could arise such as exclusion, negative judgments, rumors, physical altercations etc.) We already talked about how people can learn from their mistakes and the power of forgiveness and about "letting it go." What I would really like you to be aware of is how attached we can become to "Drama" and the attention we get from it. By "attached" I mean how tempted we might be to make a bigger deal of it and blow it out of proportion or exaggerate – our temptation to talk about what occurred with our friends, and how much we might really enjoy the attention and sympathy from our friends. While it might feel good to receive this attention at the time, remember, "Two wrongs do not make it Right." What do you think this means?"

(Allow for further discussion from members. Note: some members may talk of past situations where they felt justifiably upset for being wronged by another.)

BEING A VICTIM AS A CLAIM TO FAME

SS "It is normal to feel hurt or disappointed when someone is mean or treats us disrespectfully, but if you focus on the negativity, and make other people aware of it, and don't let it go – what do you think the likely outcome will be?"

(Allow for discussion on this topic. This is a rather heavy topic that may take some time to process. Often the secondary gain for "keeping the hurt alive" or enlisting others to share in our anger is far too tempting to not pursue. The attention or notoriety received when we play the "victim" is often too rewarding to deny. The emphasis on this concept is to alert group members that dramatizing and seeking attention through negativity usually backfires and just creates more of the same. Moreover, it depletes energy and eventually leaves us feeling weak.)

 © YouthLight, Inc.

SESSION 6

CHOOSE HAPPINESS AS THE BEST REVENGE

"I would like you each to consider the consequences of staying angry with someone and letting your friends know about your anger. Is this really a way to honor yourself? We all like our friends to support us, feel sorry for us when we are sad, but to hold onto the anger and to let it continue to spread to our friends can lead to disaster for everyone. Remember, we always do have the power to choose how we are going to react to any situation. Staying mad or upset for too long actually drains our energy. Sometimes – happiness is the best revenge! By that, I mean when we remain happy even when someone hurts our feelings, because we choose not to take it personally, or we choose to believe that the other person has a problem, we may feel sorry for them and choose to remain happy anyway – then we have really won! We get to keep our tank full, focus on being a happy person as well as being a good friend to our self and to others. We also continue to attract good things to us, instead of being stuck feeling sad or with our negative feelings."

SILENCE IS CONSENT
Taking a Stand Against Relational Aggression

It is important to engage the BFF members in a group discussion regarding the importance of not contributing towards negativity whether it is gossip, bullying – or exclusion by his or her silent participation.

Pose this question: "If you encounter a situation where another child is targeted, what should you do about it? What are your choices? If you say or do nothing and listen or go along with the negativity, do you realize that you are actually agreeing with the bully? At the very least, choose not to encourage the person (and further damage) by "sticking around" and remaining silent. By refusing to participate in any type of bullying, other kids will see your "goodness" and you will actually see that you begin to build better friendships."

SESSION 6

BUILDING RESILIENCY
(Act as though…and you will become)

Remaining calm and not allowing other people to drain our energy or cause us to feel badly, or hold onto negativity is a real skill that can be developed. In building this resilience skill, you may need practice. Practice maintaining your power and sense of well being by acting calm, upbeat, or positive. Over time, this will become natural. When you begin to see that you are still "okay" in spite of another's negativity, this skill of remaining happy will come naturally. Remember, to honor yourself. Be your own best friend.

DEALING WITH NEGATIVE ATTACKS

SS "The final step is to walk away from this experience. While you are not responsible for another person's happiness, you are responsible for your own behavior. Remember to be "friendship focused," act and be a friend first. Over time, other people will learn that you do not tolerate negativity."

This discussion teaches a powerful coping skill when/if a child encounters another who chooses to verbally criticize or berate him or her. If that occurs, it is best to be prepared. BFF members should be aware that first, it is important to make direct eye contact. Remain calm despite any negativity for approximately 15 seconds – but no more. Do not pay attention to body gestures or what is being said. Although it may be tempting to act defensively or even counter attack, do not respond with negativity, verbally or otherwise. Instead, count slowly in silence up to 15. At the same time, imagine that something wonderful is about to happen to you, (this image can be about anything fun or gratifying). After no more than 15 seconds has passed, you might respond with, a simple reply such as, "Sorry you feel that way, take care, bye. Or "If you want to talk about this later, we can, but I don't care to listen to you now. I'm sorry you are so upset." Understand that it is not what you say; it is **how you say it**! You want to say this sincerely and confidently.

SESSION 6

 ## Exercise: The Send Off

 "I would like to share an exercise with you that you can do when you have bad or sad thoughts, or if you are mad at someone and you are having a really difficult time just letting go of your thoughts. In other words, you just keep thinking about it anyway. You can do this anytime, anywhere, and with practice, it will help you to get rid of the negative thoughts!"

- First, all you have to do is see your thoughts in your head. Give your thoughts permission to leave. Then see your thoughts gently floating out of your head. You can place them in an imaginary balloon – perhaps a purple, pink or white balloon – and in your mind see all the negative thoughts fill up this balloon. Once the thoughts have been entered into the balloon and you see, in your mind, that the balloon is full, gently let go of the string and see the balloon drift way up into the sky until it is out of sight.

(Note: This balloon exercise may be experienced by using real balloons. The BFF members may write a thought on a small piece of paper such as a posted, then role the paper and place inside individual balloons. The written message may be an unwanted thought that they wish to let go of – or another version of this exercise is to focus upon a wish that needs to be sent out or released. Either, way, this is an enjoyable ritual to let go of encumbering thoughts or feelings).

- Another way that helps to let go of unwanted thoughts is to see these thoughts placed on a billowy, soft, white cloud and see the cloud carry them high into the sky and off to the heavens. Breathe deeply when you're imagining this happening. If any thoughts should return, you can repeat either of these exercises until the negative thoughts have totally vanished.

- Close your eyes and imagine replacing the space where those old thoughts were with a golden light that you send from your heart. Imagine seeing the words "love and release" as a thought while you breathe in and out.

- Feel proud of your accomplishment and happy about your choice not to keep these bad thoughts around.

SESSION 6

Exercise: Reframe Thoughts & Words

"Another way to deal with negative thoughts is to "reframe" or change the thought into a positive or neutral thought. So when we say "reframe" it means "replacement thought." Find the "Silver Lining" or the positive things about any situation, and know that whatever happens, you have the power to turn it into something good." Consider the following examples: (Slowly.......read the following sentences along with the replacement thought or reframe).

- Math is so boring. **Reframe:** Math is really a game. If I learn the rules, I know can win.

- My parents are too strict. **Reframe:** By following their rules, I know my parents eventually will trust me with more freedom.

- I don't like (So-and-so), she is so stuck-up. **Reframe:** (So-and-so) doesn't act friendly. I wonder if she is shy. I will try to get to know her by smiling and saying "Hi, So-and-so" I need to remember that I am only responsible for how I act, how I choose to look at things and how I am being.

- I am not as good as the other kids in my PE class. That is why no one wants me on their soccer team. **Reframe:** We are all better at some things than others, sometimes I even laugh at myself. All I can do is try to do my best though. If I keep trying, I will get better. By being brave, (trying something even though I am scared), at least I Know I did my best. Trying my best is just as important, and often more important than having the skills.

- I feel so embarrassed! I forgot my guitar for the recital. **Reframe:** Everyone makes mistakes. Making mistakes actually can help me to remember what not to do next time. I know I would forgive someone else who forgot their instrument. I now choose to forgive myself.

- The weather is awful and I wanted to go outside and play today. **Reframe:** This is an opportunity for me to discover a new way to entertain myself or accomplish something at home. (Think of a list of projects you have put off, or something fun to do like bake a pie, play a board game, read a good book, write letters, etc.). I accept the weather and will still have fun inside today.

SESSION 6

SS "Does anyone have other examples they can share? Does anyone have an annoying thought they would like to share or want help with to change or re-frame it?"

(Allow time for group process.)

SS "What about when you hear someone else saying something mean or hurtful about you or someone you know, then what can you do? **(Allow for group input.)** You can also reframe what someone else might say by thinking about what they have said in a different way yourself. People who say things that are mean or negative or just annoying, are usually not very happy. They do not have a very full "tank" or they do not feel like they have much power. They might want to gain attention from others. Or, they might be hurtful to someone else because they think it will make them feel better. There is an old saying, "Misery Loves Company." What that means is that when someone feels badly, they often try to bring other people down too. So they might say mean things or even want to hurt someone. Or they might want their friends to join them in feeling angry or upset. When someone says or does something unkind or mean to you or someone you know, you can remain calm and protect yourself and your feelings by thinking: "That person must be having a really bad day or that boy/girl must be feeling very hurt, angry, or sad." You should know that it usually has nothing to do with you directly. As we said before, maybe they are having a bad day, or someone else upset them and they haven't gotten over it. However, if the other person is angry with you for a good reason, that is, you know you have let them down etc., then you need to take responsibility and apologize. However, if you are just being targeted for no reason, then first "reframe" the way you are looking at this experience. Then physically remove yourself from the situation. This holds true for cell phone and internet exchanges too. Just click off your computer or cell phone."

(Allow for group discussion and practice "reframes." Group members may need to clarify this concept further.)

"Remember, we all learn from each other. We all have an opportunity to learn when we share our personal experiences. Thank you for sharing yours."

SESSION 6

CREATING AN UPLIFTING/CENTERING THOUGHT

"What happens in life is often not nearly as important as the meaning you give it. The meaning that you place on an event determines your beliefs and "colors" or affects your experience. I have found it useful to have a personal uplifting/centering thought or a quick little saying that keeps me on track, especially if I am feeling stressed. (Or you might sing a fun song in your mind.) It actually helps to put a smile on my face and I can more easily "let go" of negative feelings. My centering thought or favorite phrase is: "Keep it light and fluffy." Or perhaps you could say: "I'm better than that!" or "I am more than enough!" When I think of these words, I realize that nothing is really that terrible or bad. Remember that life is always changing, so whatever the stressful situation is, it won't last forever. Again, we always get to choose how we emotionally react to stress or disappointment. Perhaps, each of you can think of a personal thought or phrase that will serve to remind you of being okay with whatever occurs and most importantly – to not worry about future outcomes. Instead, choose to be happy now."

Exercise: Role Play – Coping with Relational Aggression

Provide opportunity for Role Playing. Have one member role play a bully and the other member role play a bystander and another role play being a target. Encourage participants to practice learned skills for maintaining energy: Zip-ups, reframing, forgiveness, compassion, positive thinking, choosing a "centering thought," etc.

SESSION 6

WHEN WE KNOW WE HAVE HURT SOMEONE
Mistakes and amends: The power of learning through experience

"We have previously talked about the idea that at one point, or another, everyone makes mistakes. Mistakes allow us to understand what we might choose to do or say differently next time, under the same or similar circumstance. Mistakes help us to understand and gain "insight" about how our words or actions might affect another person or an outcome. If you think you have made a mistake, the most important thing to remember is:

1. Take responsibility: Admit what you did wrong

2. Apologize with sincerity

3. Repair or make amends for any wrong doing

4. Learn from your mistake

5. Promise yourself not to make the same mistake again

6. Follow through on your word

7. Forgive yourself and be thankful for the lesson learned.

(Allow for a group discussion on these concepts: Discuss the meaning of sincerity, i.e. just saying "I am sorry" and meaning it is a good start; but it does not make for a sincere apology. All the above mentioned steps need to be completed).

KEEPING CALM – BEING CLEAR
The Power of the Breath

"We're going to talk a little more about how taking a few big deep breaths can give you more power. (Have BFF group members pay attention to things that happened to them today and identify how they are feeling at this moment. For example, they might be feeling anxious, bored,

SESSION 6

upset or tired. Let members know that by slow, rhythmic breathing or "Breath Work," we can calm ourselves down and feel "centered." Have everyone do this and then note how their feelings inside just changed.) This is another way to think about honoring ourselves. When we are relaxed, we feel more self-confident and we allow our own creativity and other talents to come forward. We can actually tap into knowledge and power we have already learned and may have forgotten. You might want to try this before taking a test in school or starting a sports activity or receiving a music lesson, for example. Before you begin the activity, it is a great idea to take some deep breaths, and then perhaps see a beautiful golden light surround you. Then once you have calmed yourself, and with good intention, allow your responses to come forward, easily and effortlessly. You may be amazed at how well you perform after doing that. When we are nervous or pressured, we can shrink our energy field and not perform as well. So, be aware that you can positively affect your energy level and your performance by remaining calm."

→ **Homework:** Make any journal entries regarding daily random acts of kindness you are able to do; how you choose to think about or react to a situation, apologies, forgiveness, etc. Try a reframe, create your own personal centering thought, and note situations and your responses when you've used deep breathing exercises to stay calm and relaxed.

SESSION 7

Change and Acceptance: Knowing the Difference /Personal Recovery/Compassion/Integrity/Shifting Perceptions

My Stuff... Your Stuff... and Stuff that Just Happens: Discerning where your power and influence lies.

Group Leader extends warm welcome to BFF members. Share homework assignment. Check in with group members to discuss any issues or concepts learned the previous week for clarification: Reframing negative self-talk; reframing negativity heard or received from another; apologies; forgiveness, how deep breathing worked for you. Ask members how they have "filled their tanks" this week.

Problems Are Perceptions
How To Know What You Can Influence And What You Cannot.

This discussion seeks to discern and describe how children can effectively understand what is within their scope of influence or control and what is not (consider that "Discretion is the better part of valor"). This also reiterates the idea of feeling "stuck" as being the same as feeling powerless.

SS "When we are unable to release or "let go" of negative ideas, such as feeling angry or that we've been "wronged" somehow by negative judgments or perhaps a situation that is unfair – by keeping those bad feelings alive, we are only punishing ourselves more. Likewise, it is important to understand our true sphere of influence. (To demonstrate sphere of influence, have everyone form a big circle. Then have one member stand in the middle so that no matter how far they spread their arms, they cannot touch anyone in the circle. (Explain that since the person in the middle cannot actually touch the others, they do not physically have an influence). Think of this as "a sphere of influence." There are some things we can influence physically, mentally, or emotionally, and some we cannot, and it is important to understand the difference."

 © YouthLight, Inc.

SESSION 7

"Although we cannot change another person, or necessarily change a given situation or circumstance; we may influence change by our own behavior as well as how we feel or "perceive" something. We do have the power to "shift" how we experience people and things. However, certain negative circumstances that we really cannot change, that are outside of our sphere of influence at this time, may have to be tolerated. Again, it is very important to understand that sometimes you have no power or influence. Sometimes it is necessary to "accept what we cannot change and have the wisdom to know the difference.""

"For example, have you ever seen someone who is driving get angry at another driver or become frustrated because there is a traffic jam? Or, has anyone you know, become upset when it rains or if a special event is cancelled? How about, if you are trying to go on vacation and the airplane is delayed? Are those situations that you have control over or the power to change them? While many situations can be really annoying, we need to understand which situations we really have influence or control over and which ones we do not. When we allow a bad situation to ruin our day, or cause us to feel really upset, it is like we are punishing ourselves. We are allowing our energy to be drained when there is nothing we can do about it anyway. What we can do is to always look at how we can choose to "make lemonade out of lemons" or make the most of a situation."

(Allow for group discussion on the meaning of this lesson.)

- Encourage BFF group members to consider how they can best manage a negative situation. This may include "reframing"; releasing or letting it go; turning it into a more positive opportunity; staying in gratitude; or realizing what can be gained or learned from it.

SESSION 7

PERSONAL RECOVERY
SOMETIMES DOING THE RIGHT THING HURTS

SS "Doing the right thing is not always fun or pleasant. Sometimes making the right choice can be hurtful. Sometimes doing the right thing is uncomfortable, or it takes a great deal of courage. Sometimes doing the right thing can make us feel lonely. This is true especially when our "friends" want to do or be something that we disagree with or know is not right. We all want to be liked and accepted. We all want to have friends and be popular. However, if we go along with what someone else wishes or what a group of kids want to do or "pressure" us to do and we know it is wrong – we will lose our self-respect. And that is not something that feels very good when it happens. All of us know what is right and what is wrong or not okay when something happens or is said. And, with practice, over time you will find that it becomes easier and easier to do the right thing or at least always follow through with good intentions." When we honor this, and we do the right thing (even when it is really hard because our "friends" will be mad or we think we will miss out on something, or other kids will reject us or make fun of us), I promise, you will grow to be a much stronger, more powerful and a happier person – because you have "Integrity." Does anyone know what the word "Integrity" means?"

(Allow group member input regarding this concept. Encourage members to share their experiences with this. And encourage members to share how it felt when they did something they knew was wrong).

Group Leader: Share the Definition of Integrity
1. Moral or ethical strength: character, honesty, principle.

2. The quality of being honest: honesty, honor, upstanding; incorruptible.

In other words, it means that you are honest about your feelings and how you deal with things.

 © YouthLight, Inc.

SESSION 7

MAINTAINING TRUST THROUGH COMPASSION and INTEGRITY

Group Leader: It is important to share the concept (in your own words) that while we may have challenges because of difficult experiences and life may even seem unfair or disappointing at times, by believing in yourself and by trusting that goodness will prevail, anyone can live a life of grace and compassion toward others. Everyone can choose to live a life demonstrated by acts of kindness, generosity, being aware, being grateful, being open to improving even when it's uncomfortable or difficult, with honor and respect for yourself and others.

JUST WALK AWAY...

"We have talked about "Peer Pressure" and how we need to stay in our "Integrity." We need to be true to ourselves and to "do the right thing." If you see your peers acting in mean ways, or saying something to hurt someone, do not join in. Do not stand around and watch. Never empower bad behavior. You should just walk away. If everyone stopped paying attention to negative drama what do you think would happen?

Now, if someone is being physically threatened or hurt, it would be best to go find a teacher or responsible adult and tell them about the situation."

(Allow for BFF group discussion.)

SESSION 7

 ## Exercise: "GET YOUR SHINE ON"

*Note: There are two separate versions to this particular exercise.
One version is designed for girls and the other is for boys:

Have the BFF group members form a circle and instruct them to gently close their eyes. (If you have some soft, low, gentle music, you may turn it on.) Have members begin calm, relaxed breathing. Direct members to breathe in the following way:

1. Slowly, deeply, breathe in counting to seven, Hold your breath for count of seven, then breathe out for count of seven.

2. Practice this breathing exercise for approximately seven breaths.

Next: Encourage the members to envision the following scenario:

SS "Pretend that you are arriving at school tomorrow morning. As you walk onto the school campus, other students, friends, and teachers, all greet you with warm smiles. They are all thinking about how much they admire you, really like you, and even how they wish they were just like you. Start to think about what words they might be thinking. How would you like everyone to think of you? What is it you would really like others to love and appreciate about you? Take a few minutes just "seeing" this scene in your mind."

(Allow a few minutes for members to reflect upon this experience.)

Group Leader: Direct the following:

SS "Begin to "feel" what this is like. Feel your energy growing from your heart space. See these special words, these words of praise – words that describe how truly wonderful you are, or how you would like to be seen or thought of. I will tap on (name a member's) shoulder, and when I do, he/she will say a word that comes to mind in this experience."

Once the first word is said then the member seated on the right says their positive word, and we will continue going around the circle so each of you has a chance to say a positive word that comes to your mind. This can be a word or phrase that you feel really good about or that describes you.

- Group leader then taps on a member's shoulder and begins this process. After two or three rounds of words expressed by each group member, the group leader will end this by saying, "Okay, very good – thank you. Keep your eyes closed and start to think of these amazing words we all have heard. See the words floating above us and moving through our group."

- After a few moments, the group leader will direct the following: "Now think of a color, a color that just seems right for you. It could be your favorite color, or it could be a color that just feels pleasant for now. See that color grow brightly in your mind's eye. This color then turns into a large piece of cloth – it is your own cape. This cape might be shiny, short, or long and flowing. It's your cape, so you get to decide."

- Boys Group: Describe the cape as similar to an action hero (Superman, Robin Hood, Batman etc.).

- Girls Group: No need to describe the cape further unless reference to royalty or someone famous is made.

NEXT: The group leader continues with the following visualization: "Now, remember those amazing words we spoke of a little while ago? See those words floating around us, slowly, like a carousel, moving around and through our group." (The group leader may restate some of the words that were spoken earlier by the members….reminding them of the different words of praise.)

Boys Group: "See the words that you really like, the words you would like other people to think of you as being. As you "see" a word you like, see it fall into your cape. Each desired word that is floating, as you choose it, simply drops down and sticks magically onto your cape."

"Once you have all the words you want on your cape, then see them become brighter and empowered. You might see a lightening bolt of energy strike your cape as it is now quite powerful."

SESSION 7

Girls Group: "See the words that you really like, the words you would like other people to think of you as being. As you "see" a word you like, notice that a golden needle and thread appears in your hand. As you see the words you desire, see each word fly onto your magic golden needle. You quickly and easily sew these beautiful words into your cape. The golden thread empowers each word and secures each word."

"Once you have all the words you want applied to your cape, then let's add some bling! See rubies, sapphires, diamonds, emeralds, pearls, and crystals. Your amazing cape is taking on a whole new look. It is so very beautiful. It is so very powerful."

NEXT: The group leader instructs the members to (in their mind) put their amazing cape on. To tie it around their neck and with outstretched arms, gather this wonderful cape around them, as if they're hugging themselves. "Once you are wearing your special cape, I want you to feel the words in the cape. These words are becoming a part of you, a part of who you really are. Feel how that feels—and know that you can be all of this. You are amazing, you are admired, you can be any way you choose." We're going to call imagining yourself wearing your cape "Getting Your Shine On."

NEXT: The group leader makes the following suggestion: "So now that you have access to your own wonderfulness, because as we already learned, we always choose how we are acting or being – if you happen to have a bad day, if you happen to forget how special you are, if you see one of your BFF group members is having a difficult time, is sad, or he/she feels badly, you can always remind yourself or your friend to "GET YOUR SHINE ON" and you or they will know exactly what you mean. This cape and all that it means is always available to you. It is a power you can always tap into. Now slowly and gently open your eyes."

SESSION 7

(Allow for group discussion on this exercise. Students seem to really enjoy this exercise and may make statements during the process such as "I can really feel it" Or "Oh, my gosh" or "Wow, I feel so different" etc. If this should occur, continue to affirm and agree they are amazing, strong, awesome etc.) Again, this discussion should be led with the notion that we choose how we feel about ourselves. Sometimes, when we are feeling down, or we have forgotten our greatness, our energy collapses. In order to "Keep our Tank Full," we need to have positive and powerful ways to build and maintain our energy.)

→ **Homework:** Journal random acts of kindness and compliments. Think about staying strong under peer pressure. Practice "acting happy, confident, and positive." Remind yourself to walk away from negative people and events. Practice your breathing exercise. Remember to "Get Your Shine On."

*Ask group members to bring a personal photo and/or one or two family photos that they really like (with their parents permission) for the BFF Session #8 project.

SESSION 8

FINAL BFF GROUP MEETING

Creating a Dream: The Art & Power of Creating a Personal Vision Board / Considering Pearls of Wisdom / Recapping the total BFF Group experience.

Share homework assignments and any journal entries students wish to volunteer.

<u>**Final Group Exercise:**</u> **Celebrating You - Creating a Vision Board**

> "Vision without action is a dream. Action without vision is simply passing time. Action with vision is making a positive difference."
> –Joel Barker

Vision boards are a fun and creative way for students to "dial into" or define their goals, as well as what they appreciate about themselves and their life. The vision board can serve to remind the BFF members to be in gratitude. Another important feature of the vision board is that it allows one to focus more upon a personal goal or intention, or what they imagine for themselves. This may involve what they are creating for the future (maybe they plan to go to college or travel, etc.) and/or what they aspire to have or be. The more defined or finite one's goals are, the better chance that the goal will be realized. It is most helpful to have a definite, detailed plan of action. The vision board serves to remind each member to stay on course. More than that, it imprints a message, and energetically sends out a desire for how they wish to be, and, as previously mentioned, what they wish to strive for or create.

<u>Vision Board Group Exercise</u>

Preparation: Supply BFF members with the following materials:
- Poster boards (one each)
- Magazines (a variety of magazines suitable for children)
- Colorful/decorative stickers
- Glue sticks (one each)

SESSION 8

- Personal photographs
- Paper cutting scissors
- Markers / fine tip felt pens
- Paints for artwork
- Pastel crayons
- Colored paper

Instruct the BFF members to create their own poster or vision board, by cutting out pictures or words, with any or all of the following elements:
- What you enjoy about your life
- What you like about yourself
- What you are grateful for
- What qualities you respect in yourself and others
- What is important to you
- What you would like to create more of in your life such as friendships; future goals; fun experiences –vacations, hobbies, talents, learning something new etc.

This is an open project, there are no rules; this is each BFF member's own personal and positive vision of their life and/or what they would positively like to attract or create in their life. Allow the group members the enjoyment of this exercise. You might provide soft background music if possible. While the members are involved in this creative design project, you might read the following philosophical statements. After reading each quote out loud, pause and allow for group members' input and discussion:

1. "Optimism is the faith that leads to achievement. Nothing can be done without hope and confidence." – Helen Keller

2. "Life is partly what we make it, and partly what is made by the friends we choose."
   – Tennessee Williams

3. "The basic difference between an ordinary man and a warrior is that a warrior takes everything as a challenge; while an ordinary man takes everything as either a blessing or a curse."
   – Carlos Casteneda

SESSION 8

4. "No one can go back and start a new beginning, but anyone can start today and make a new ending." – Maria Robinson

5. "To a happy person, the formula is quite simple: Regardless of what happened early this morning, last week, or last year – or what may happen later this evening, tomorrow, or three years from now – now is where happiness lies." – Richard Carlson

6. "Care inspires and gently reassures us, lending us a feeling of security and support. It reinforces our connection with others. Not only is it one of the best things we can do for our health, but it feels good – whether we are giving or receiving it."
   – Doc Childres and Howard Martin

7. "You must be the change you wish to see in the world." – Mahatma Ghandi

SHARE VISION BOARDS

When members have completed their vision boards, they may wish to share their board with the rest of the BFF group. Some members may need more time to work on their vision boards at home. Instruct members to keep their boards at home and display them where they can view their board each day. Allow each BFF member to share their completed vision boards with the group. Encourage each member to talk about what they appreciate or are grateful for, and what they aspire to or envision having in their life. Discuss short- and long-term goals and the possibility of creating what one desires.

> **"To change yourself, you need to use imagery, emotion, and repetition. Do all three and virtually anything is possible."**
> **– Dr. Joe Vitale**

Remind them that they can each create more positive experiences in life by first having a desire or "intention" clearly expressed: by speaking it, writing it down, envisioning and feeling it in their heart – as though it is happening or has already happened; then by taking action, feeling joyful and maintaining the vision.

 © YouthLight, Inc.

SESSION 8

It is important to understand that our goals or heart's desires must also be released when need be. Explain that any time we are too attached to an outcome; then realizing a goal can actually be delayed or restricted. For example, just as it is important to study for exams, if we become anxious, fretful or worry a lot about our grade on the test, we may actually "freeze up" and forget the answer! On the other hand, if we are prepared, if we desire to be successful, and we relax with confidence during the exam, most likely, a better grade will be achieved. Our lives are a path toward learning the true sense of happiness. That happiness emerges from within. When we really trust and are able to "let go" then that which we desire or something even better will occur. As a result, a true opportunity for success is created.

RECAPPING THE BFF GROUP EXPERIENCE:

• The group leader will thank and personally acknowledge each member for their participation in the BFF group.

• Ask group members to share what they have learned or enjoyed over the past eight weeks of BFF group sessions.

• Recap /Group discussion on the following concepts:
Respect/Honor/Integrity
Mind/Body/Emotion Connection
The Power of Choosing (reactivity, perceptions)
Random Acts of Kindness
Giving/Receiving Compliments
Forgiveness/Apologies
Releasing – Letting go of negative thoughts or drama
Reframing
Body Language
Building/Protecting personal power (keeping your "tank" full)
Gratitude
Power of Change vs. Acceptance

 © YouthLight, Inc.

SESSION 8

Walking Away
Self-calming /Breathing Exercise
"Get Your Shine On"
Creating a Vision
Kindness/Compassion

CLOSING THE BFF GROUP

The group leader may choose to issue a "Certificate of Completion" to each member and acknowledge how much their presence positively impacted the whole group experience. (A special treat such as cake and ice cream may be shared as a way of celebrating the efforts and commitment of the group.)

Remember to "Be Friendship Focused" by being a friend first.

Follow Up

POST-BFF GROUP PARENT/TEACHER MEETING

This is an opportunity to invite parents and teachers to share what points or lessons were covered during the past eight week BFF group sessions. It is also an opportunity to invoke a broad sharing and discussion from both teachers and parents regarding any progress made or particular concerns that remain.

The BFF group leader may share the various concepts or insights and group processes covered over the course of the group. This should include how to cope with relational aggression by creating and maintain a strong sense of personal power and resiliency.

Inform parents and teachers that they may follow-up with a short scheduled telephone conference in order to address any current issues with their child or student. Thank each parent for allowing their child to participate in the BFF group and thank the BFF Group Members for their contributions to the group's experience.

Optional: BFF Leader may wish to supply a handout of other community resources that offer individual/group/or family counseling support.

Optional: BFF Group Members may be invited to this meeting in order to share their completed vision boards with the group. At the end of the 8-week group encounter, possibly one or two members may benefit from or desire to continue participating in the next newly formed BFF group. You may consider allowing this by appointing those members to the role of "Mentor Assistant." This will provide opportunities to review previously learned concepts and skills as well as maintain continued social/emotional support, while making them feel special.

Meeting is adjourned!

BFF: Crossword Puzzle

Name: _____ Date: _____

BFF: Crossword Puzzle

Across:

1. soften, soothe, peacefulness, tranquil, serene,
2. bravery, fearless, heart, valor, fortitude, the quality of mind enabling one to face danger or difficulty
4. The seat of a person's innermost emotions and feelings
5. deep, thorough or mature understanding: insight 2. The ability to make sensible decisions: 3. That which is known; discovered; perceived
7. a condition of supreme well-being and good spirits : blessedness, bliss, cheerfulness, joy
8. without equal or rival, incomparable, first and last, one and only
9. being grateful: appreciation, gratefulness, thankfulness, thanks
11. absolute certainty in the trustworthiness of another: confidence, dependence, faith, reliance, trust: conviction, feeling, idea, opinion
13. the combination of emotional, intellectual, and moral qualities or attributes that distinguishes a person
15. a statement of acknowledgment expressing regret or asking a pardon
16. to have a high opinion of; admire; respect; value
19. moral or ethical strength, character, the quality of being honest
20. to regard with great pleasure or approval; to have a high opinion of; respect, value; honor
21. capable of being depended upon : dependable, reliable, responsible, solid
22. no false appearance, honest, true

Down:

1. the power or quality of attracting; magnetism
2. full of polite concern for the well-being of others : attentive, courteous, thoughtful
3. the ability to recover quickly from sadness or discouragement; flexible, adaptive, able to bounce back
6. clear, free, unblocked, approachable
10. to give or impart physical, emotional, or mental vitality
12. a person whom one knows, likes, and trusts
14. the act of choosing; the power or right of choosing; an option
17. the quality of being honest : moral or ethical strength : character
18. A declaration that one will or will not do a certain thing: assurance, pledge, guarantee, word of honor

Possible Answers:

admire, apology, belief, calm, character, charisma, choice, considerate, courage, energize, friend, gladness, gratitude, heart, honesty, honor, integrity, open, promise, resilience, sincere, trustworthy, unique, wisdom

BFF: Crossword Puzzle KEY

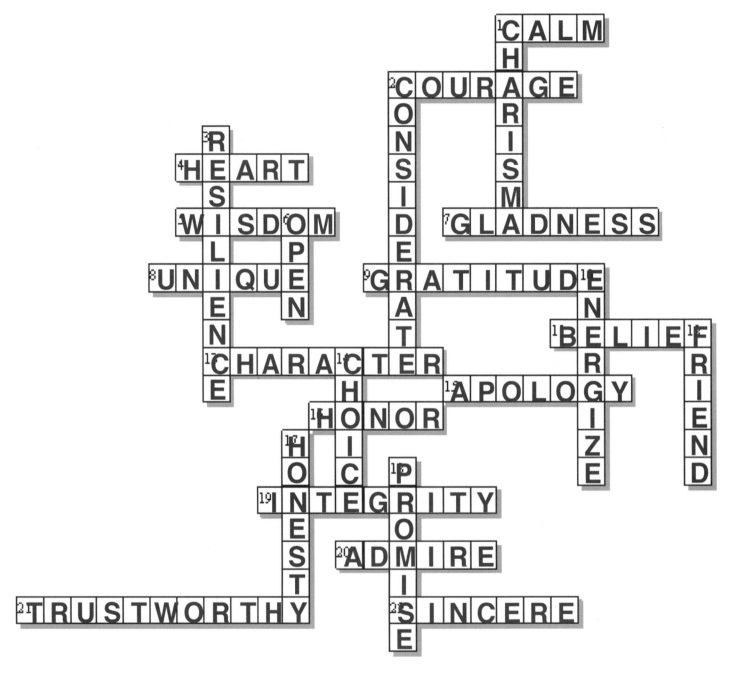

The crossword puzzle key contains the following answers:

CALM

COURAGE

CHARISMA

RESILIENCE

HEART

WISDOM

OPEN

GLADNESS

UNIQUE

GRATITUDE

ENERGIZE

BELIEF

FRIEND

CONSIDERATE

CHARACTER

CHOICE

APOLOGY

HONOR

HONESTY

INTEGRITY

PROMISE

ADMIRE

TRUSTWORTHY

SINCERE

BFF: Be Friendship Focused

PARENT PERMISSION FORM

The BFF support group's goal is to help children to discover new ways to formulate and maintain healthy peer relationships. An improved sense of personal empowerment is met by shifting perceptions, increasing awareness, and learning compassionate communication skills that build positive relationships. BFF is an anti-bullying prevention /intervention. Groups are forming at

_____ (location) to begin on _____ (1st session date) through _____ (last session date). The BFF group is scheduled to meet each _____ (day of the week) at: _____ (time) for a total of eight (8) sessions. The group facilitator is

_____ (name). Parents will participate through periodic ratings or feedback. Snacks may be provided.

I give permission for my child _____ (name) to participate in the BFF support group. I understand that confidentiality will be maintained within the group unless there is a perceived safety risk.

You may contact _____, the group leader, at _____ (phone number) if you have questions.

_____   _____
Parent Signature   Date

_____   _____
Parent Signature   Date

BFF: Be Friendship Focused

INITIAL PARENT SURVEY

Your child,_____, is a member of the social skills support group, BFF: Be Friendship Focused, held at _____ (name of school or meeting place) from _____ (1st group session date) and _____ (last group session date). The focus of this group process is to encourage better social skill development through an improved self-concept. Not only is this a self-empowering experience, but an opportunity for members to enrich their lives through education, improved self-perception, and receive life-long tools to further insure personal success.

In order to better address your child's particular needs and assess with his/her progress, kindly complete the enclosed survey:

1. Please describe your child's personal or unique strengths including skills, talent, character traits:

2. Is your child experiencing any particular emotional stress? Indicate any areas of concern regarding your child's ability to be successful (this may include social, emotional, health, educational, or other background issues):

If you have any questions, please contact the group facilitator (name) _____ at _____ (contact phone number). Thank you for returning this form at your earliest convenience.

BFF: Be Friendship Focused

A SOCIAL SKILLS SUPPORT GROUP CONFIDENTIALITY AGREEMENT

I AGREE TO MAINTAIN CONFIDENTIAL INFORMATION THAT MAY BE SHARED BY FELLOW PARTICIPANTS. I WILL BE RESPECTFUL OF OTHERS INCLUDING LISTENING AND PARTICIPATING IN ALL ACTIVITIES AND ASSIGNMENTS. I UNDERSTAND THAT SHOULD I NOT COMPLY OR BREAK CONFIDENTIALITY, I MAY NOT BE ABLE TO PARTICIPATE FURTHER.

I AGREE TO COME TO EACH SESSION FOR A TOTAL OF 8 WEEKS.

Group Facilitator: _____

Group Members: _____

_____

_____

_____

_____

_____

_____

_____

_____

_____

_____

_____

Kristine Rose Grant is a licensed marriage and family therapist, certified relational coach, and school psychologist. In her private practice, Kristine specializes in helping children and families to strengthen connections and resolve conflicts. As a relational coach, Kristine guides and supports individuals towards building and maintaining healthy relationships. Kristine also has a unique inspirational letter-writing service known as "Inspired Heart Ink" dedicated toward empowering personal relationships through the written word. (Refer to her website at www.inspiredheartink.com for more details.)

As a school psychologist, Kristine has dealt with countless children who are challenged by various learning difficulties that may include emotional or social setbacks. According to Kristine, "All too often it seems that our children have lost their sense of safety and connection without knowing the meaning of wholesome family values. As family dynamics become more fragmented and parents or care takers are less available, and as school and community resources dwindle, the long-term, devastating effects upon our children's emotional growth and well-being are witnessed. Every child yearns for acceptance, appreciation, and a sense of belonging." This BFF: Be Friendship Focused manual provides clear step-by-step guidance and an opportunity to make a difference for our youth and for our future.

"Finding the beauty and joy
that is always available
and choosing a brighter path
allows us each to live in
a state of grace."